Advance Praise for

"This Cartoon Book—Banda Dessinada—is Remarkable, Powerful, Incisive, Accessible, Dramatic, Marxist, Revolutionary, Generous—like the man himself—Peter McLaren. Brought to Life! A Revolutionary Document! Wow! Zap! Kapow! Peter McLaren—remarkable global revolutionary activist educator—brought to full-colour life. Brilliant combination of McLaren's Life, Influences, Education Politics, Fire and Poetics with the Cartoon/Comic form. But this ain't no Cartoon Character! A Revolutionary Document!"

Dave Hill, UK Marxist activist and Educator

"ZAP! POW! KABOOM! Here is a life story destined to be made into a comic book---the only medium wide and weird enough to capture the complex, dynamic, multidimensional, generative, shifting, and creative force that is Peter McLaren. Read this book and be inspired to dive into the contradictions, to launch your own voyage of discovery and surprise, to have your blooming in the noise and chaos of the whirlwind."

Bill Ayers, author, *To Teach: The Journey, in Comics*

"The indomitable Peter McLaren is the living embodiment of critical pedagogy, a truly radical educator who has always been interested in stretching the limits of genre to explore, innovate and communicate. In the comic *Breaking Free* we see his ability to reinvent himself and communicate himself and his ideas afresh. That's why we all love him."

Michael A. Peters, Distinguished Professor at Beijing Normal University, China, Emeritus Professor in the Faculty of Education at the University of Illinois, Urbana-Champaign

"Albert Einstein once said that a life lived in the service of others is a life worth living. Now comes the story of Peter McLaren. The life and times of this renowned radical educator, as recounted in these engaging pages, holds up a mirror in whose reflection we see the great aspirations of our age. At once a piece of art, social criticism, and critical pedagogy, here is a portrait of the contemporary struggles of the oppressed, told to the backdrop of McLaren's biography. Nothing less than a modern epic!"

William I. Robinson, Author of *Into the Tempest: Essays on the New Global Capitalism*

"McLaren's led a politically and intellectually rich—and entertaining—life, which is renewed through this compelling graphic novel. Each page is filled with important and relevant lessons we would do well to heed as we struggle for peace and justice."

Derek R. Ford, DePauw University, Indiana

"A valuable sort of "McLaren for Beginners" in which Peter offers his own Pedagogy of Hope in the stylistic tradition of Zap Comix! The resulting graphic memoir is a radically socialist and countercultural portrait of a life imaged both as and on behalf of the attempted humanization of the world. Critical pedagogy by any means necessary..."

Richard Kahn, Ph.D., Antioch University, Los Angeles

"A wonderfully colorful, creative, radical, and lively way to bring together the lived history of an individual with the larger historical struggle for a more just world—indeed a revolutionary message for our times."

Antonia Darder, Leavey Endowed Chair in Ethics and Leadership, Loyola Marymount University

"Peter McLaren is one of the leading architects of contemporary critical theory, a radical activist, a storyteller, a revolutionary Marxist humanist, a scholar of liberation theology, the poet laureate of the educational left, and much more. In the face of his tremendous achievements, *Breaking Free:*

The Life and Times of Peter McLaren, Radical Educator avoids the trap of representing Peter as a classical comic hero. Instead, its authors weave a warm story about a working-class boy who has risen to become his own type of hero: an intellectual hero, a hero of humility and respect for everyone, who inspires and gently pushes people to do the best of their ability for the benefit of humankind. *Breaking Free: The Life and Times of Peter McLaren, Radical Educator* is a superb biographical sketch aimed at those who know little about Peter's work, an eye opener for those who read Peter's works but never met him in person, and an important contextualisation for those who seek deeper understanding of relationships between Peter's works and the person behind them. With this extraordinarily important book, Peter McLaren once again crosses the well-entrenched border between 'serious' scholarship and popular culture and insists that the path to emancipation and freedom belongs to everyone."

Petar Jandric, Zagreb University of Applied Sciences, Croatia

"Globally esteemed and erudite critical pedagogy icon McLaren, once again breaks new ground, collaborating with illustrator Miles Wilson, creating an autobiography that is one and the same time a Manifesto for a socialist alternative to capitalism. The images, darkly humorous, present a serious challenge for a new generation of youth."

Bernardo Gallegos, Professor, National University, Los Angeles

"*Breaking Free: The Life and Times of Peter McLaren, Radical Educator* is a unique and important new publication. It is a beautiful compliment to his theoretical, philosophical, empirical and activist writing and engagement on the ground. It helps to fill in the story. It shows us how his life, thinking and work have been influenced, over the years, by other important colleagues, comrades and activists. In the spirit of Ruis' ABChé, this is a must-read for undergrads, graduate students, scholars and all who seek to make this world a better place."

Marc Pruyn, co-editor, *The Peter McLaren Reader, Volumes I & II*

"A comic book! A comic book! But there's nothing really comic about this graphic autobiography by one of our era's most creative philosophers of education. After branching out from Paulo Freire to liberation theology, Peter McLaren's poetic genius and astounding imagination have outdone themselves here with "Pow!", "Crash!", and "Bang!" that will leave readers inspired, breathless and smiling with delight."

Mike Rivage-Seul, Emeritus professor of Peace and Social Justice Studies, Berea College

"How was the radical educator educated? Find out here, as Peter McLaren leads us through the liberatory labyrinth of his life—from Toronto to San Francisco, Chiapas to Caracas, Azania to Anatolia, UCLA to the PRC. Meet his superhero comrades from Hugo Chavez to Che Guevara's daughter. Sail with him as he tacks between the turbulent tides of his allies Timothy Leary and Allen Ginsberg. Meet the teacher's teachers—Umberto Eco and Michel Foucault, Paolo Freire and Joel Kovel. The script is Professor Xavier meets The Invisibles. The illustrations are The Yellow Submarine meets Fantastic Planet, and/or Dragonball Z meets Transmetropolitan. Look out Avengers and Justice League! Breaking free of the artificial scarcity on superpowers, UCLA's most dangerous professor is here, armed with critical pedagogy and Marxist spirituality, to fight against bad schools and bad government, and to help us all join the revolution against the capitalist world-system and its national security states."

Quincy Saul, author/editor of *Truth and Dare: A Comic Book Curriculum for the End and the Beginning of the World*

BREAKING FREE

BREAKING FREE

THE LIFE AND TIMES OF PETER MCLAREN, RADICAL EDUCATOR

WRITTEN BY Peter McLaren
ILLUSTRATED BY Miles Wilson

Myers Education Press

GORHAM, MAINE

Copyright © 2019 | Myers Education Press, LLC

Published by Myers Education Press, LLC
P.O. Box 424 Gorham, ME 04038

Myers Education Press is an academic publisher specializing in books, e-books and digital content in the field of education. All of our books are subjected to a rigorous peer review process and produced in compliance with the standards of the Council on Library and Information Resources.

Library of Congress Cataloging-in-Publication Data available from Library of Congress.

13-digit ISBN 978-1-9755-0169-3 (paperback)
13-digit ISBN 978-1-9755-0170-9 (library networkable e-edition)
13-digit ISBN 978-1-9755-0171-6 (consumer e-edition)

Printed in the United States of America.

All first editions printed on acid-free paper that meets the American National Standards Institute Z39-48 standard.

Books published by Myers Education Press may be purchased at special quantity discount rates for groups, workshops, training organizations and classroom usage. Please call our customer service department at 1-800-232-0223 for details.

Visit us on the web at **www.myersedpress.com** to browse our complete list of titles.

CONTENTS

PREFACE

It was a perfect fall day in the sunny city of Orange in Orange County, California, for hatching the idea for this comic book. Antique cars paraded around the Old Town plaza, lowriders parked beside a local funeral home, the inglorious fools in City Hall made merry with real estate barons, when I was confronted by a Nazi in the washroom of Orange City Hall, who pronounced me the most hated man in the city, shortly before his buddy clicked open his switchblade, menacing those in the council chambers. Chapman students filed into the coffee shops, bikers rode by with Pepe the Frog emblems emblazoned on their helmets, and residents of the homeless encampment near Angel Stadium were poaching oranges from the trees outside of the public library.

Numerous friends, colleagues and critics whom I have entertained with stories of my teaching and political activism over recent years have often encouraged me to publish an autobiography. They would tell me that recounting some of my experiences working with radical educators around the world would be a necessary contrast to the contemporary din of political unthought here in the U.S. I doubt that I will ever write an autobiography, and this comic book will likely be the closest thing to the genre that I will ever publish. And I am fine with that. This book has mainly been written for those who have engaged my work over the past thirty years. But it has also been created to reach the millennial generation who has grown up with comics and graphic novels, who are comfortable with the format, and have developed a discerning appreciation of illustrated text, and yet who know nothing of my work or that of other socialist educators.

My life has been full of hurdles that many of us face due to our human frailty, the choices we make and the synchronicities that, in retrospect, we have come to realize have shaped our lives in important ways. It is these moments of retrospection that I have tried to conjure into life through the creative brilliance of a young illustrator, Miles Wilson. Miles is a graduate student at Dodge College that is affiliated with Chapman University, where I now teach. When Miles showed me samples of his animated work, I knew he was the perfect person to illustrate the key events in my life that appear in the pages that follow. The general arc of the comic depicts my life, from its early working-class beginnings in Toronto, to my hippie days, some of which I spent in San Francisco and Los Angeles, and back to Canada where I taught elementary school for five years in a notoriously violent area of North York. Miles also illustrates my move into the academy where I discovered radical new ways of teaching students to become critical, active agents of social change. The most insistent philosopher that graced my life was Paulo Freire, the great Brazilian educator, who was imprisoned for teaching peasants in Northeastern Brazil in such a way that the peasants began to achieve a critical consciousness about their past, present and future lives. And, finally, Miles recounts my encounters with revolutionary philosophers and teacher activists worldwide, as I began to see the world in a very different light than during the days of my conservative and conventional upbringing. I came to see the lives of the oppressed as stories of self-reliance demonstrated in the people's war against the transnational capitalist class. This transnational capitalist class is not a cabal of bankers in tailcoats and top hats who demand factory workers routinely kiss the whip, but often politically indifferent, family loving individuals who are joined by common interests of augmenting vast fortunes through corporate power while making sure that the conditions for reproducing such wealth remain unhindered. Following in their wake are the echo chambers of the far right and the burgeoning infrastructure for fascism. All social problems have a simple solution: it's the immigrants, the GLBTQ cadres, the Black Lives Matter movement, the feminists, the politically correct. This is what happens when the economic takes over the political, when we are reduced to what job we have, to whatever means we have to eke out a living.

The last thing I wanted to do was to romanticize my life, and Miles' brilliantly dark, comic approach to his work effectively effaces any glint of self-aggrandizement on my part. The challenge for Miles was to prevent his dark humor from becoming too satirical, distracting from or impeding the seriousness of the ultimate goal of the book—which is to provide some insight into the life of a radical educator, a life fraught with crucial challenges that have serious consequences for other people, a life often surrounded by lurking aggression, a brutal homogeneity, surreal episodes that can be baffling, amusing, and deadly serious—all at the same time. I wanted to produce a book for a younger generation, a book that they can appreciate on its own terms yet, at the same time, can be used by teachers with their students, and in teacher education classes in university settings. Miles was more than up to the task. His artistic signature was able to reveal inner layers of my experiences left fallow by words alone.

The book chronicles my journey as an only child living in a working-class neighborhood of Toronto who decides after graduating from university to become an elementary school teacher. After five years of teaching students from grades two through six at a school in a public housing area of North York, Ontario, the notebook I kept to maintain my sanity was published by a major outlet. The notebook was in diary form and, like a highly stoked fire, it became a runaway best seller in Canada in 1980. You could purchase it on book stands at subway entrances. There were attempts to put together an HBO and Canadian Broadcasting Corporation made-for-television-movie, a project which fell through at the eleventh hour due to a technician's strike (I bear no hard feelings toward the strikers, good for them!). The name of the book was eventually changed from *Cries from the Corridor* to *Life in Schools*, after it was republished in the United States, and after adding theoretical sections to the book to explain how poverty under capitalism devastates some communities more than others, and does so disproportionally with respect to race, class, gender. *Life in Schools* became a popular book among progressive and radical teachers and is still widely used in teacher education programs across campuses in North America, and is especially relevant during times of soaring income inequality. My experiences teaching working-class students, snapshots in which I was mired in the moment in the long-dissolved microcosmos of the school, constitute a major section of the book.

This is the first attempt to give my elementary experiences a predominately visual context. I left it up to Miles to decide which episodes to illustrate from my elementary school diary. But the book moves beyond those classroom experiences to demonstrate my evolution as a scholar and activist, and my decision to take the academic path less traveled through a serious engagement with Marxist scholarship and revolutionary political activism. There were some life-changing (and life-threatening) moments in the journey following my days as an elementary school teacher as I traveled throughout Latin America, met barefoot doctors, guerilla fighters, community activists and radical teachers, many of whom became mentors. There were to be more learning experiences in Europe and Southeast Asia, totaling visits to thirty countries. Ultimately Miles was given free rein to select and interpret events in my life, injecting them with a dark, hallucinatory realism and wildly humorous approach. This book would have been impossible without him.

That I have managed to survive as a professor in a university without having to give up my Marxist philosophy or my approach to my Catholic faith, which is marinated in liberation theology, is a mystery to some, especially given the stubborn obstacles radical educators face in universities that are steadily becoming corporatized. I chose the comic book format as an innovative means of combating the current unctuous charlatanism that passes as educational reform and as a way to shift the stagnant education policy debate not just to the left but in the direction of a broader struggle for a socialist alternative to capitalism. The U.S. has destroyed socialist forces in Vietnam, Cambodia, Laos, Philippines, Guatemala, Haiti, Ecuador, the Congo, Brazil, Dominican Republic, Chile, Angola, Grenada, Nicaragua, Bulgaria, Albania, Afghanistan, Yugoslavia, El Salvador, and it has marched many more countries to the gallows of forced austerity and misery. Have you been forced to witness your mother being raped? Have you been forced to watch your father flogged? Have you tried to fight for your freedom with shackles on your legs? Have you been hung by a cotton screw, forced to wear a tin mask, made to sleep with an iron collar with protruding spikes? Are you constantly girding yourself to face another day without food?

Indigenous peoples described European settler colonialists as having a forked tongue, like a snake. Contemporary U.S. fascism is powered by our current president Trump's tongue that works as a blivet, a poiuyt, a devil's tuning fork. It is sequestered in Twitter rants that incant a perfervid white nationalist state with the oily charisma of a carnival barker. The process of moronization and stupidification unleased by the mass media has taken hold of the collective archetypal power of aggression that works in the service of the dictatorship of capitalism. Dark powers have arisen from the shards of a capitalism in crisis, and they are us. We are broken beings, commodified bundles of labor power helpless against a whirlwind of terror. This pedagogy underwriting this comic book is designed to pry us free from the white-knuckled grasp that capitalism has on our belief that there is no viable alternative.

Fascist ideology is not something that burrows its way deep inside the structural unconscious of the U.S. from the outside, past the gatekeepers of our everyday psyche; rather, it is a constitutive outgrowth of the logic of capital in crisis that can be symptomatically read in the ways we treat our fellow citizens, in the ways we have built a surveillance state, in the ways we have priced working-and-middle-class citizens out of medical insurance, in the ways we have fomented racialized hatred of immigrants working in hotels, restaurants, and manufacturing and food-processing plants, and in the ways we have demonized refugees from America Latina who are trying to find refuge from the violence in those countries that U.S. capitalism has held in debt peonage for so many decades of ruthless economic dependency. Capitalism is a system in which brutality is a necessity, so much so that true democracy refuses to descend there. It has prevailed over socialism not because it is a better system but because of the power of the military industrial complex supporting it, along with CIA covert ops. It is an auction block in which souls are destroyed in the service of profit. It discharges such a stench of injustice that even the most dung-loving flies will not condescend to visit.

That this comic book will be considered subversive is a given, although there is nothing intrinsic about the comic book genre that guarantees that its fans will take to the barricades in support of socialism. Fans of swing music among the Hitler youth risked a trip to a concentration camp for being decadent and subversive, such as belting out lines from songs such as the Flatfoot Floogie—"Oh the flat foot floogie with the floy floy"—moving along the street with one of their crepe-soled shoes on the curb and one on the road—but I suppose any genre of popular culture could accommodate Trumpmania. Yet at the same time educators should not dismiss the power of the comic book to cultivate robust challenges to capitalist hegemony, to capitalism's irreconcilable differences between means and ends affecting the fate of the entire planet earth. This means proletarianizing higher learning by integrating word and world and combining socialist ethics with classroom practice, all the while anticipating a world in which every person has free access to and distribution of goods, capital and services, captured by the famous slogan "From each according to his ability, to each according to his needs," popularized by Karl Marx in his 1875 Critique of the Gotha Program.

I certainly could augment from my notes further development of some of these themes but space considerations unfortunately prevail. The genre of this book requires that it be punctuated by a rapid journey through experiences which at the time seemed ruinously paralyzing and unreal. As I began to reflect upon them, I recognized that my experiences were, in effect, not unreal at all but overly saturated with reality. My story is undoubtedly filtered through the visual signature of Miles, who brought layers--at once humorous, dark, and self-reflexive--of his own experiences and understandings to the finished artwork. The final outcome will, I hope, provoke readers to rethink education not as a set of classroom practices but rather come to see teaching as the journey of a lifetime, as a way of being and becoming, as a political project for building a socialist alternative for ourselves, our students, and for the future.

Peter McLaren

ACKNOWLEDGMENTS

I would like to thank Miles Wilson for his unyielding support for this project and for sharing with educators his profound artistic talents. I would also like to thank Chris Myers, whose editorial vision is precisely that vision we need for today, for encouraging this work, and for his sage advice along the way. And finally, a thank you to my wife, Yan Wang, for teaching me so much in the winter years of this long and rambling life.

Peter McLaren

I've met so many people in my life, but none that have encouraged me to pursue my love of the arts and help become the person I am like my mother—who never said "no" to me, my Father—whose movie marathons and trivial knowledge of film led me to create my own, and my grandparents. Chris Myers, Peter McLaren, and everyone at Myers Education Press for giving me this wonderful opportunity, and finally...

...everybody else who knows me (you all know exactly who you are) and/or knew me.

Miles Wilson

PART ONE

EARLY LIFE

I WAS BORN AT TORONTO GENERAL HOSPITAL INTO A WORKING CLASS FAMILY.

MY OFFICIAL NAME WAS "PETE", BUT MY DAD CALLED ME "BUSTER".

THE CONCEPTION OCCURRED THREE YEARS AFTER MY FATHER LARRY RETURNED FROM WORLD WAR II, WHERE HIS COMPANY—THE ROYAL CANADIAN ENGINEERS—FOUGHT THE NAZIS FOR SIX YEARS.

THAT WAS A LONG TIME TO BE AWAY FROM MY MOTHER FRANCES, WHO WROTE HIM EVERY DAY.

2.

MY DAD NEEDED THREE YEARS TO GET HIMSELF RE-CONDITIONED TO CIVILIAN LIFE AFTER THE WAR BEFORE.

IN 1939, MY UNCLE TERRY HAD JOINED THE ROYAL NAVY AS A NAVIGATOR.

HE FLEW IN A FAIREY SWORDFISH OFF THE HMS ARK ROYAL AND HELPED LOCATE AND SINK THE GERMAN BATTLESHIP BISMARCK.

HE WAS A HERO—AND HAD A MEDAL PINNED ON HIM BY KING GEORGE VI...

...YES, THE KING WHO STAMMERED.

MY PARENTS TRIED TO HAVE ANOTHER CHILD, BUT MY MOTHER HAD A TUMOR REMOVED FROM HER UTERUS AND WAS NOT ABLE TO CONCEIVE AGAIN.

SO HERE I WAS, AN ONLY CHILD IN A CONSERVATIVE WORKING-CLASS FAMILY WHO ALWAYS TOLD ME I WAS GOING TO BE THE NEXT PRIME MINISTER OF CANADA— REPRESENTING WHAT WAS CALLED THE PROGRESSIVE CONSERVATIVE PARTY.

I ALWAYS THOUGHT THE WORD "PROGRESSIVE" WAS INTENDED AS A JOKE.

I ATTENDED THE LOCAL ANGLICAN CHURCH AND SERVED AS A CHOIR BOY.

MY FAMILY MOVED TO WINNIPEG WHEN I WAS ELEVEN.

WINNIPEG
WELCOME BIENVENE
ONE GREAT CITY!

I WOULD FIGHT WITH THE LOCAL ITALIAN KIDS —WAS NOT MUCH OF A BOXER, BUT HAD A GREAT HEADLOCK THAT WOULD NEARLY POP THE EYEBALLS OUT OF MY OPPONENTS.

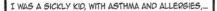

I WAS A SICKLY KID, WITH ASTHMA AND ALLERGIES,...

...BUT PLAYED FOOTBALL IN JUNIOR HIGH SO I COULD DATE SOME OF THE CHEERLEADERS.

MY OWN EXPERIENCES OF THE EDUCATIONAL SYSTEM ARE HOUSED IN THE COLD CHAMBERS OF MEMORY.

AS ONE OF THE FIRST STUDENTS AMONG MY PRIMARY SCHOOL CLASSMATES TO ENTER THE ROOM EACH DAY, I WAS WELCOMED BY ROW UPON ROW OF CHAIRS STACKED UPSIDE DOWN ON DESKS—WHAT LOOKED LIKE VARNISHED, WIND-WORN BONES OF LONG-VANISHED CREATURES.

IN THE FOGBOUND REACHES OF MY MIND, I CAN STILL RECALL THE PUNGENT STENCH OF THE CLEANING FLUID USED TO WIPE AWAY THE UNDEVIATING ANXIETY OF THE SCHOOL DAY, BUT I CANNOT RECALL THE FACE OF A SINGLE TEACHER PRIOR TO MY JUNIOR HIGH YEARS,...

...SAVE ONE "SHOP" TEACHER WITH A JACK-O-LANTERN RICTUS WHO STRUCK ME REPEATEDLY ON TOP OF MY HAND WITH A METAL RULER, BRUISING ME TO THE BONE.

THE BLEAK ARCHAEOLOGY OF THE SETTING AND THE THREAT OF TEACHER VIOLENCE KEPT ME UNCOMFORTABLY ATTENTIVE,...

...WHICH WAS ITS PURPOSE.

8.

I NEVER COULD GET ALONG WITH THE ARGUS-EYED CAPTAINS OF THE LAW— EVER VIGILANT ABOUT POLICING OUR DESIRES, MONITORING OUR FANTASIES, AND CREATING THE SCENARIOS FOR US TO PRESENT OURSELVES IN EVERYDAY LIFE.

IN 1967, I HAD BEEN WALKING DOWN YONGE STREET IN WILLOWDALE WITH SOME FRIENDS, TRIPPING ON SOME WEED.

TWO COPS GRABBED ME WHILE MY FRIENDS SCURRIED DOWN THE ALLEY.

THEY THREW ME IN THE SLAMMER THAT NIGHT...

GODDAMN HIPPIE!

CRACK

THWACK

STOMP

SNAP

...AND BEAT ME WITH THEIR METAL FLASHLIGHTS.

ONE NIGHT, I VENTURED OVER TO THE CAROUSEL BALLROOM ON VAN NESS AVENUE—NOT FAR FROM WHERE I WAS CRASHING WITH SOME HIPPIES.

THE GRATEFUL DEAD WERE PLAYING, BUT JUST AS INTERESTING, I MET AN EX-HARVARD PROFESSOR NAMED TIMOTHY LEARY— WHO TOOK QUITE A SHINE TO ME THAT NIGHT.

13.

FIVE YEARS EARLIER, DR. LEARY HAD BEEN EXPERIMENTING WITH PSILOCYBIN AND LSD —TAKING IT ALONG WITH SOME OF HIS STUDENTS AND RESEARCH SUBJECTS.

HE WAS BECOMING KNOWN AS "THE HIGH PRIEST OF LSD", AND ADVOCATED THAT YOUNG PEOPLE "TURN ON, TUNE IN, AND DROP OUT."

SOUNDED GOOD TO ME AT THE TIME.

WANNA STUDY ABROAD FOR A BIT? TRY *THIS*. A GENTLEMAN NAMED "OWSLEY" MADE IT HIMSELF.

14.

15.

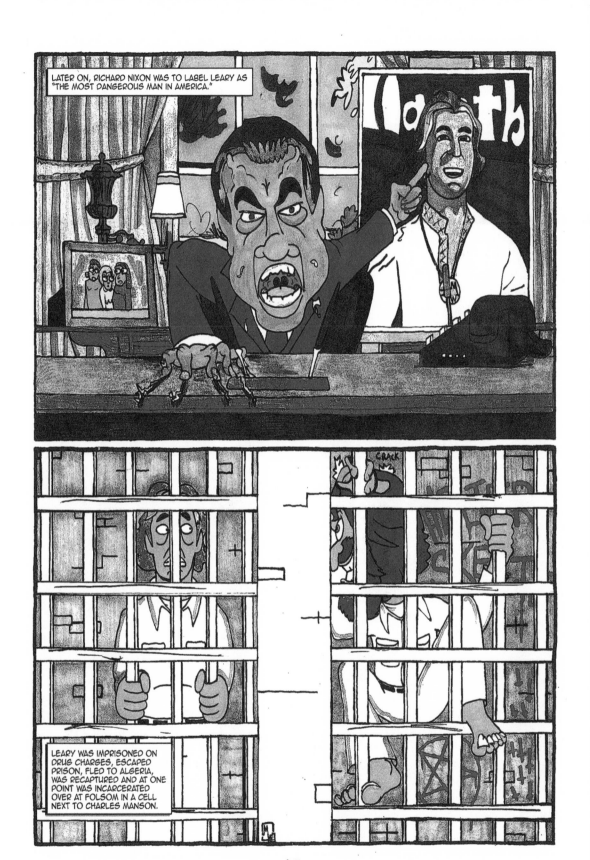

LATER ON, RICHARD NIXON WAS TO LABEL LEARY AS "THE MOST DANGEROUS MAN IN AMERICA."

LEARY WAS IMPRISONED ON DRUG CHARGES, ESCAPED PRISON, FLED TO ALGERIA, WAS RECAPTURED AND AT ONE POINT WAS INCARCERATED OVER AT FOLSOM IN A CELL NEXT TO CHARLES MANSON.

17.

SHORTLY AFTER LEAVING SAN FRANCISCO, I MET UP WITH THE POET ALLEN GINSBERG— WHO TOLD ME TO STOP TAKING DRUGS AND CONCENTRATE ON MY WRITING.

NOW I FELT THAT I WAS OFFICIALLY PART OF THE BEAT GENERATION.

GINSBERG GAVE ME THE CONFIDENCE TO START THINKING OF MYSELF AS A WRITER.

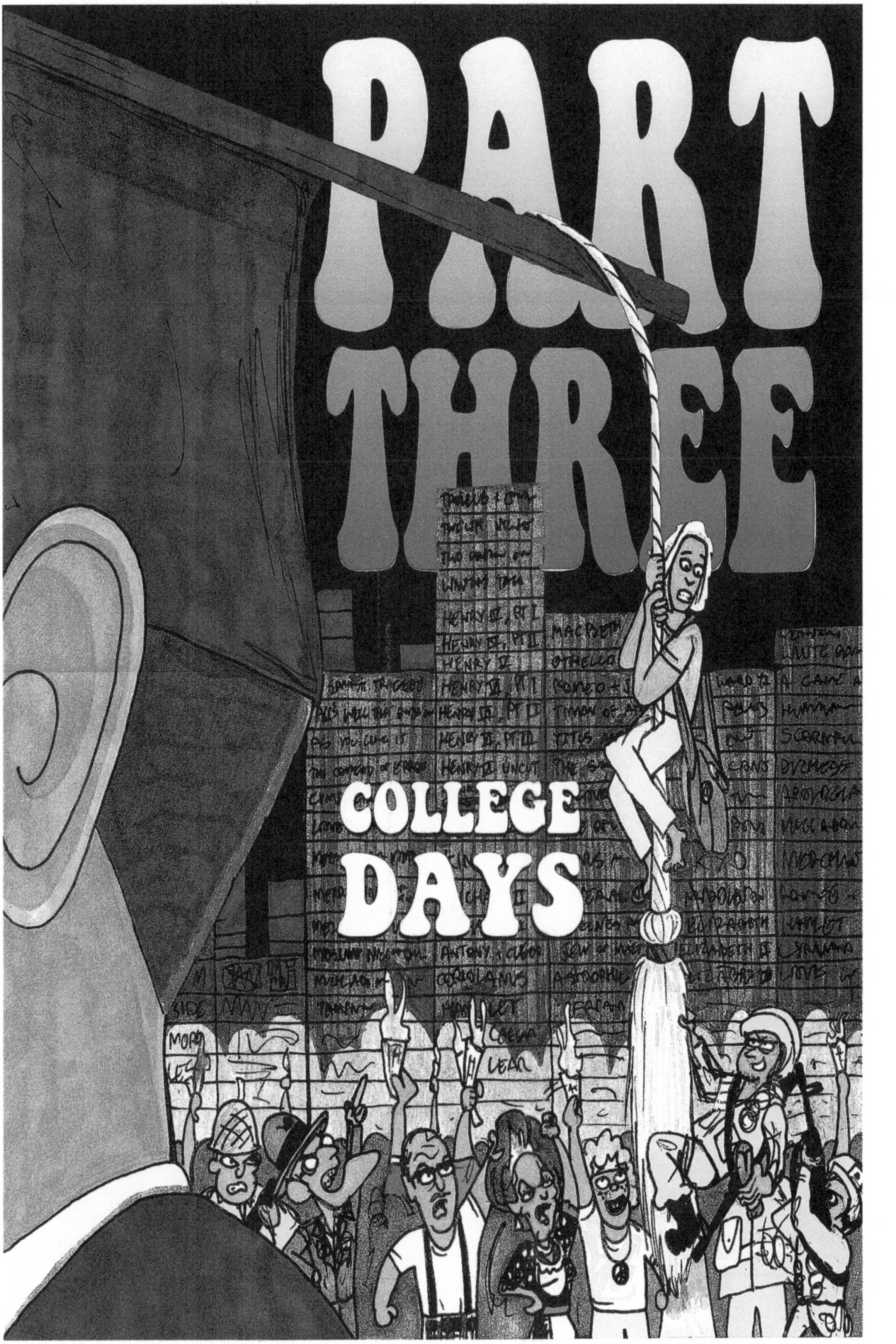
PART THREE
COLLEGE DAYS

WHEN I RETURNED HOME, I STARTED TAKING CLASSES AT THE UNIVERSITY OF TORONTO,...

...PICKING UP SOME BLUES GUITAR LICKS FROM JOHN HAMMOND, JR. AT THE RIVERBOAT CAFE,...

Riverboat

NOW APPEARING JOHN HAMMOND, JR.

...AS WELL AS LUKE AND THE APOSTLES FRONTMAN MIKE McKENNA—

I CAN STILL REMEMBER WATCHING McKENNA'S HANDS PRANCE GRACEFULLY ALONG THE FRETBOARD OF HIS FENDER STRATOCASTER LIKE DEER IN A FIELD.

I WAS ALSO OFFICIALLY TAKING GUITAR LESSONS WITH DAVID WILCOX.

20.

BEING BORN DEAF IN ONE EAR WASN'T A BIG HELP TO MY GUITAR PLAYING, AND BESIDES THAT, I HAD LITTLE NATURAL TALENT.

SO, I STARTED READING OLD AND MIDDLE ENGLISH AND ELIZABETHAN DRAMA...

...BUT I DIDN'T FORGET ABOUT THE VIETNAM WAR.

DURING MY UNDERGRADUATE YEARS, I HELPED DRAFT RESISTORS WHO HAD HEADED UP TO TORONTO.

MOST OF THE COUNTRY SAW THEM AS TRAITORS.

I SAW THEM AS PATRIOTS.

CREEEEEK

FUMBLE

21.

IT MADE ME ANGRY TO LEARN THAT PEOPLE OF COLOR WERE BEING DISPROPORTIONATELY RECRUITED IN THE INFANTRY—AND WERE MORE LIKELY TO BE SENT TO THE FRONT LINES.

I LEARNED ABOUT THIS THROUGH SOME FOLKS THAT CALLED THEMSELVES THE BLACK PANTHERS.

I WAS IMPRESSED WITH WHAT THEY STOOD FOR...SPECIFICALLY WITH ANGELA DAVIS, BOBBY SEALE, AND HUEY P. NEWTON—THREE OF THE GROUP'S MOST PROMINENT MEMBERS.

I ALSO HEARD THAT DOZENS OF STUDENTS WERE PROTESTING THE WAR OVER AT THE UNIVERSITY OF BERKELEY AND WAS DETERMINED TO GO *THERE*.

I STAYED IN SOME FLOP HOUSES NEARBY AND EVEN SLEPT IN A CHURCH BASEMENT FOR A WHILE.

DURING THE DAYS, I WOULD READ MY POETRY AND GIVE OUT MY CANADIAN ADDRESS TO YOUNG PEOPLE WHO WERE THINKING OF HEADING UP NORTH AS A RESULT OF THE VIETNAM WAR.

I DIDN'T THINK MY FRIENDS IN CANADA WOULD BELIEVE WHAT I WAS DOING WHEN I GOT BACK AND SHARED MY STORIES, BUT ONE THING'S FOR SURE...

...I KNEW MY PARENTS WOULD BE UPSET.

A BLACK WOMAN I MET ON A BUS SHOWED ME HER COPY OF THE AUTOBIOGRAPHY OF MALCOLM X.

MALCOLM X WAS A REVOLUTIONARY WHO HAD BEEN ASSASSINATED IN 1965.

I STARTED READING ABOUT MALCOLM X—AND MARTIN LUTHER KING, JR... WHO WAS ALSO KILLED JUST THREE YEARS AFTER MALCOLM.

...AND I WAS IN LOS ANGELES—EXPLORING THE COUNTERCULTURE OF SUNSET BOULEVARD AND LAUREL CANYON—WHEN I HEARD THAT ROBERT KENNEDY WAS KILLED.

I DECIDED TO HEAD BACK TO TORONTO AND FIGURE OUT WHAT TO DO NEXT.

24.

WHEN I RETURNED FROM MY ADVENTURES IN THE HIPPIE BARRIOS OF THE UNITED STATES, I BEGAN LISTENING TO A LOT OF FOLK AND BLUES MUSIC—SPECIFICALLY WOODY GUTHRIE'S "THIS LAND IS YOUR LAND", BOB DYLAN'S PROTEST SONGS, AND THE MUSIC OF ROBERT JOHNSON AND MUDDY WATERS.

THIS KIND OF MUSIC HELPED ME UNDERSTAND MY OWN WORKING-CLASS HISTORY AND GET MORE OF A CRITICAL GRASP OF THE INEQUALITY, RACISM AND VIOLENCE THAT RUNS RAMPANT IN CAPITALIST SOCIETY.

IT HELPED ME REALIZE THAT THIS IS OUR SOCIETY—FILLED WITH MANY CULTURES, AND NOT ALL OF THEM ARE TREATED EQUALLY.

I SUPPOSE THAT OLD MAN TRUMP KNOWS JUST HOW MUCH RACIAL HATE HE STIRRED UP IN THAT BLOOD-SPOT OF HUMAN HEARTS WHEN HE DRAWED THAT COLOR LINE HERE AT HIS BEACH HAVEN FAMILY PROJECT.

IN 1950, WOODY GUTHRIE WROTE A SONG ABOUT THE RACISM LURKING WITHIN FRED TRUMP—FATHER OF OUR "PRESIDENT" DONALD TRUMP—WHEN HE WAS LIVING IN A BUILDING IN BEACH HAVEN AND LEARNED THAT TRUMP ONLY WANTED WHITE TENANTS.

WOODY'S GUITAR HAD A SIGN ON IT THAT READ, "THIS MACHINE KILLS FASCISTS."

I MADE A SIMILAR SIGN FOR MY GUITAR.

I SPENT CONSIDERABLE TIME WITH A VARIETY OF COLORFUL AND CREATIVE INDIVIDUALS WHOSE LIVES BOUNCED PARADOXICALLY BETWEEN EXPRESSIVE RITUALS OF EMANCIPATION AND PATHOLOGICAL RITUALS OF SELF-DESTRUCTION...

...BUT I DON'T THINK I'VE EVER MET ANYBODY QUITE LIKE ZEKE.

26.

SUMMER 1966

I HAD SEEN HIM AROUND THE SCHOOL. EVERYBODY KNEW ABOUT ZEKE. HIS ECCENTRICITY WAS STRAPPED ON LIKE A CODPIECE AS HE INCESSANTLY STALKED AND CHALLENGED OUR COZY CONVENTIONS.

FOR REASONS I DIDN'T UNDERSTAND YET, I WANTED TO KNOW HIM...

HAVE YOU READ PYNCHON?

I DON'T KNOW HIM.

HOW ABOUT GENET? YOU HAVE TO READ OUR LADY OF THE FLOWERS.

I'M NOT INTO CATHOLIC LITERATURE.

WELL... I CAN SEE YOU'RE UNEDUCATED. WE'LL JUST HAVE TO DO SOMETHING ABOUT THAT.

...AND SO I DID.

27.

THE FIRST WOMAN THAT I WAS ROMANTICALLY DRAWN TO WAS KNOWN AS "THE MAGIC RABBIT LADY", WHO TAUGHT ME THE SECRETS OF THE OCCULT AND HOW TO ROLL A GOOD JOINT...

...BUT THAT'S ANOTHER STORY FOR ANOTHER ADVENTURE.

29.

SO, I GRADUATED FROM THE UNIVERSITY IN THE EARLY SEVENTIES, HUNG UP MY LOVE BEADS AND MY BELOVED FATIGUE JACKET, FESTOONED OVER THE YEARS WITH SLOGANS AND HAND-STITCHED DOVES, AND ENROLLED IN TEACHER'S COLLEGE.

MY FIRST JOB WAS AT A MIDDLE SCHOOL IN A WEALTHY VILLAGE OUTSIDE OF TORONTO. AS MUCH AS I LIKED THE STUDENTS AND ENJOYED TEACHING, I FELT DISPOSABLE...

...AND LET ME TELL YOU WHY.

THOSE STUDENTS—ALREADY FAVORED WITH WEALTH AND SOCIAL POWER—WOULD PROBABLY GET BY IN THE WORLD IN SPITE OF THEIR TEACHERS; THEIR AFFLUENT BACKGROUND ALMOST ASSURED THEM SUCCESS IN THE SYSTEM.

I READ REPORTS THAT THE MOST COMMON FACTOR ON WHETHER YOU GET INTO COLLEGE IS NOT INTELLIGENCE, CREATIVITY, OR HARD WORK, BUT WHERE YOU STAND IN THE CAPITALIST SYSTEM.

OF COURSE, THERE WERE EXCEPTIONS...

...AND THOSE WERE THE ONES YOU READ ABOUT IN THE MEDIA.

36.

37.

38.

39.

40.

41.

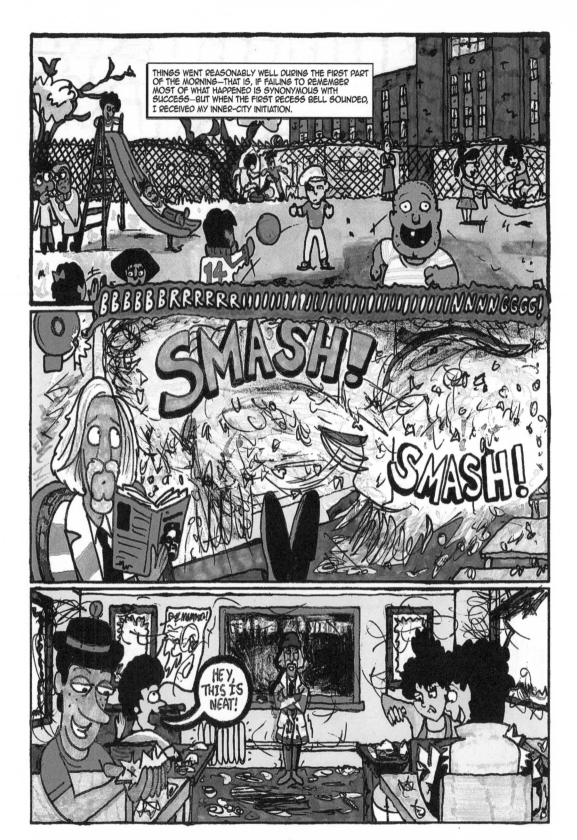

44.

46.

TUESDAY, JANUARY 18TH

ONE OF THE MORE COLORFUL CHARACTERS AROUND THE SCHOOL WAS A TWELVE-YEAR-OLD NAMED "BUDDY".

HATED AND FEARED—ESPECIALLY BY THE OTHER TEACHERS, BUDDY LITERALLY RAN THE SCHOOL, A ROLE HE PLAYED WITH THE VIRTUOSITY OF AN ARTIST.

HE WAS A MASTER TECHNICIAN WHEN IT CAME TO CREATING HIS OWN IMAGE. AT A MOMENT'S NOTICE, HE COULD BECOME A LOVER, FIGHTER, THE CHAMPION OF FREEDOM, THE KING OF THE SIDEWALKS, OR THE DEFENDER OF DANCE. EVERYTHING...AND *EVERYONE* WAS A POINT OF REFERENCE FOR HIS ACT.

THE KIDS IN THE SCHOOL CONSIDERED BUDDY TO BE A DEMIGOD. WHENEVER HE WALKED DOWN THE CORRIDOR AND SAID "MOVE OVER!", THE KIDS MOVED... AND *FAST*. HIS VOICE WAS RARELY LOUD, BUT IT HAD A WAY OF SLICING THROUGH THE AIR LIKE COLD STEEL.

BUDDY WAS WHAT YOU'D CALL A "FLOATER". FLOATERS ROAMED THE HALLS AT WILL AND WERE IGNORED SO LONG AS THEY DIDN'T LEAVE THE BUILDING. TO QUALIFY AS A FLOATER, YOU HAD TO BE INCORRIGIBLE, BUT IN A SOFT, ALMOST UNDERSTATED WAY. YOU HAD TO CONCEAL YOUR VIOLENT TENDENCIES AND RESERVE IT ONLY FOR STRATEGIC SHOWDOWNS. OTHERWISE, THE ADMINISTRATION WOULD SEND YOU OFF TO THE "OUTSIDE" OR TO ANOTHER SCHOOL.

FRED HAD WARNED US THAT BUDDY MIGHT MAKE A SURPRISE APPEARANCE IN OUR CLASSROOMS. WHENEVER HE DID, IT DIDN'T GET MORE UNNERVING THAN TO SEE HIM STANDING AT YOUR DOORWAY... QUIETLY CONJURING UP WAYS TO BREAK THE DAILY MONOTONY.

BUDDY WAS THE MASTER OF THE UNSPOKEN. HE MOSTLY TALKED WITH HIS EYES, BUT HIS FAVORITE GESTURE WAS TO YAWN LOUDLY...

...AND HERE I WAS THINKING I COULD KEEP HIM AT BAY WITH A FLARE OF MY NOSTRILS AND A CURL OF MY LIPS.

BOY, WAS I WRONG.

47.

BUDDY ALSO RAN A PROTECTION RACKET, WHERE HE AND HIS LACKEYS WOULD APPROACH A KID IN THE CORRIDOR AND DRAG HIM INTO THE NEAREST WASHROOM.

ONCE INSIDE, THEY WOULD THREATEN TO REARRANGE AN ARM, LEG, OR FACE UNLESS MONEY WAS "DONATED" TO BUDDY THE NEXT DAY.

IT WAS A NICE LITTLE EMPIRE THAT WAS CUT SHORT WITHIN A MONTH AFTER POLICE CONFISCATED WELL OVER A HUNDRED DOLLARS.

WHERE DO YOU LIVE? WE'LL TAKE YOU HOME.

TAKE ME TO NOVA SCOTIA.

FRIDAY, FEBRUARY 11TH

...AND THEN THERE WAS DUKE—OTHERWISE KNOWN AS THE "CLASSIC DUDE" TO HIS CLASSMATES.

HORDES OF STUDENTS WOULD SOMETIMES TRAIL BEHIND HIM, SHOUTING "HEY, DUKE!" OR RHYTHMICALLY CHANTING HIS NAME. EVEN TEACHERS HAILED HIM. HIS MANNER WAS ALWAYS ENGAGING.

DUKE WAS THE ULTIMATE BULLY ON THE PLAYGROUND. HE WAS SUSPENDED AFTER CRACKING A KINDERGARTENER IN THE FACE AND THROWING HIM AGAINST A FENCE... AMONG A HOST OF OTHER THINGS.

WHEN DUKE'S MOTHER GOT WIND OF WHAT HAPPENED, SHE WAS WAITING FOR HIM WITH A HAIRBRUSH.

AT TEACHER'S COLLEGE, THEY TOLD US TO LAY DOWN THE RULES ON THE VERY FIRST DAY AND STICK TO THEM...

...BUT ONE DAY I HAD THAT PUT TO THE TEST ONCE DUKE WALKED INTO CLASS.

THERE'S NO EATING IN THIS ROOM, SO PUT THE SANDWICH AWAY.

FIGURES.

I AIN'T HAD BREAKFAST, SO I'M JUST FILLIN' UP EARLY ON MY LUNCH.

WHAT DO YOU MEAN?

JUST GIMMIE TWO SECONDS!

50.

THURSDAY, MARCH 3RD

WHEN I RETURNED HOME FROM WORK, I USUALLY WENT STRAIGHT TO THE DEN AND KEPT THE DOOR SHUT FOR THE REST OF THE NIGHT. TO BIDE MY TIME, I HALFHEARTEDLY STARTED WORKING ON A SERIES OF CHILDREN'S STORIES THAT WERE ABOUT THE REAL WORLD AS OPPOSED TO THE WORLD OF MAGIC AND MAKE-BELIEVE—BUT AFTER ABOUT AN HOUR...THAT STARTED DEPRESSING ME, TOO.

MY ONLY OTHER OUTLET WAS PLAYING A BOTTLENECK GUITAR AFTER SOME OF THE DELTA BLUES ARTISTS THAT WERE BASED OUT OF THE MISSISSIPPI REGION IN THE EARLY 1920S.

IT GAVE ME A TREMENDOUS EMOTIONAL RELEASE.

51.

54.

AT THE END OF THE DAY, KIDS OF ALL AGES POURED INTO MY ROOM. BUDDY WAS THE LAST TO ENTER. I FIGURED IT COULDN'T BE TOO BAD. AFTER ALL, I STOOD NEARLY SIX FEET AND WEIGHED ONE HUNDRED AND SIXTY-FIVE POUNDS.

BUDDY WAS A TWELVE-YEAR-OLD KID, EVEN IF HE WAS BIG FOR HIS AGE.

EVERYONE WAITED IN SUSPENSE AS WE TIED OUR GLOVES ON. THEN...

55.

AFTER A FEW ROUNDS, I WAS STARTING TO RUN OUT OF GAS AND DECIDED TO END THE MATCH GRACEFULLY BY SAYING I HAD TO LEAVE FOR A COURSE.

YOU'RE OKAY.

56.

THURSDAY, JUNE 2ND

DUKE BUMPER-HITCHED A RIDE ON MY VAN SO MANY TIMES THAT ONE DAY —ON MY WAY TO LUNCH—I DECIDED TO MIX IT UP A LITTLE.

HEY, DUKE! HOW'RE YOU DOIN? WHAT DO YOU SAY YOU AND I GO AND GET A HAMBURGER?

SURE, MAN, AS LONG AS YOU'RE BUYIN'.

57.

58.

59.

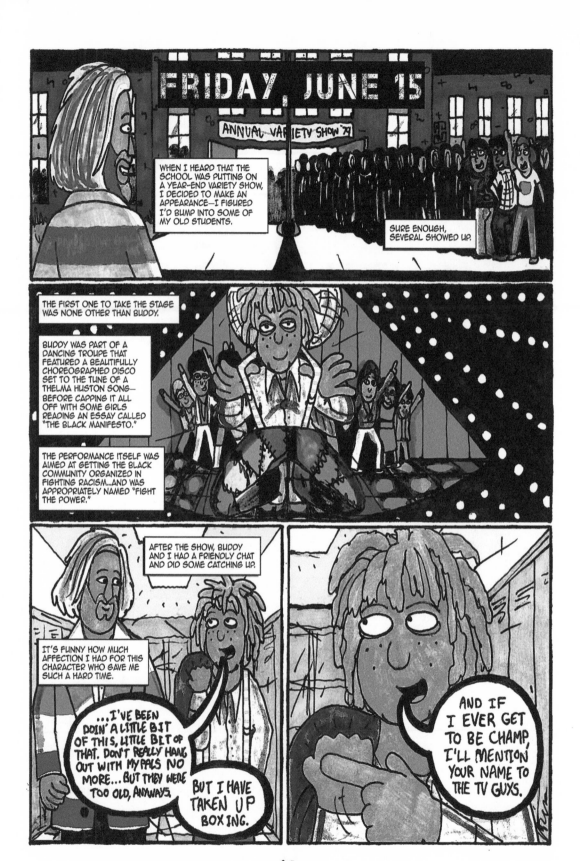

FRIDAY, JUNE 15

ANNUAL VARIETY SHOW '79

WHEN I HEARD THAT THE SCHOOL WAS PUTTING ON A YEAR-END VARIETY SHOW, I DECIDED TO MAKE AN APPEARANCE—I FIGURED I'D BUMP INTO SOME OF MY OLD STUDENTS.

SURE ENOUGH, SEVERAL SHOWED UP.

THE FIRST ONE TO TAKE THE STAGE WAS NONE OTHER THAN BUDDY.

BUDDY WAS PART OF A DANCING TROUPE THAT FEATURED A BEAUTIFULLY CHOREOGRAPHED DISCO SET TO THE TUNE OF A THELMA HUSTON SONG— BEFORE CAPPING IT ALL OFF WITH SOME GIRLS READING AN ESSAY CALLED "THE BLACK MANIFESTO."

THE PERFORMANCE ITSELF WAS AIMED AT GETTING THE BLACK COMMUNITY ORGANIZED IN FIGHTING RACISM....AND WAS APPROPRIATELY NAMED "FIGHT THE POWER."

AFTER THE SHOW, BUDDY AND I HAD A FRIENDLY CHAT AND DID SOME CATCHING UP.

IT'S FUNNY HOW MUCH AFFECTION I HAD FOR THIS CHARACTER WHO GAVE ME SUCH A HARD TIME.

...I'VE BEEN DOIN' A LITTLE BIT OF THIS, LITTLE BIT OF THAT. DON'T REALLY HANG OUT WITH MY PALS NO MORE...BUT THEY WERE TOO OLD, ANYWAYS.

BUT I HAVE TAKEN UP BOXING.

AND IF I EVER GET TO BE CHAMP, I'LL MENTION YOUR NAME TO THE TV GUYS.

60.

61.

63.

1980

TEACHING STUDENTS FROM GRADES TWO ALL THE WAY THROUGH TO GRADE EIGHT FOR FIVE YEARS TOOK ALL MY STRENGTH, AND I FELT IT WAS TIME TO PUT MY WRITING SKILLS TO THE TEST. SO, I SAT DOWN AT MY ELECTRIC TYPEWRITER AND TYPED UP REFLECTIONS THAT I HAD SCRIBBLED FOR YEARS INTO A BUNCH OF OLD NOTEBOOKS THAT RECOUNTED MY TEACHING EXPERIENCES AND CALLED IT "CRIES FROM THE CORRIDOR".

I SENT IT TO A LITERARY AGENT AND—TO MY SURPRISE—NOT ONLY MADE THE CANADIAN BEST-SELLER LIST,...

...BUT TOOK ME ON A CROSS-COUNTRY TOUR FROM HALIFAX TO VANCOUVER, WHERE I MADE AN APPEARANCE ON MARGARET TRUDEAU'S TV SHOW...

...AND SEVERAL RADIO SHOWS.

DESPITE ALL THE PRAISE AND ATTENTION THE BOOK WAS GETTING, I STILL COULDN'T HELP BUT FEEL UNFULFILLED.

I MEAN, HERE I WAS DOING ALL THIS PRESS BUT LACKING ANY REAL THEORY TO BACK IT UP.

ACTUALLY, THERE WAS SOME RUDIMENTARY THEORY THROWN IN, BUT THE PUBLISHER TOLD ME TO REMOVE IT, SAYING 'WITHOUT THE THEORY, THE BOOK WOULD BE A BEST-SELLER.'

NEEDLESS TO SAY, THEY WERE RIGHT...

...BUT AT WHAT COST?

I REALIZED THAT WHILE MY BOOK MAY'VE GIVEN A VIVID DESCRIPTION OF MY STUDENTS, IT LACKED TWO FUNDAMENTAL THINGS: AN EXPLANATION FOR WHY THOSE KIDS WERE SO FEROCIOUS, AND A MUCH DEEPER ANALYSIS OF STRUCTURAL RACISM AND CLASS WARFARE IN OUR CAPITALIST SOCIETY.

IN THE WORDS OF BRAZILIAN LIBERATION THEOLOGIAN DOM HÉLDER CÂMARA:

WHEN I GIVE FOOD TO THE POOR, THEY CALL ME A SAINT. WHEN I ASK WHY THEY ARE POOR, THEY CALL ME A COMMUNIST.

65.

PART SIX

GRADUATE STUDY

I KNEW I HAD SOME SERIOUS THEORETICAL WORK TO DO, AND IF THAT MEANT ENROLLING IN A PH.D. PROGRAM AT THE ONTARIO INSTITUTE FOR STUDIES IN EDUCATION, THEN SO BE IT.

AT LEAST I WAS ABLE TO AUDIT A CLASS WITH MICHAEL FOUCAULT— A VISITING PROFESSOR AND WHOSE WORK IS STILL VERY MUCH IN VOGUE TODAY.

I WAS IMPRESSED BY HIS WORK, BUT THERE WASN'T A SINGLE THEORY OF RESISTANCE TO CAPITALISM THAT I COULD PUT MY FINGER ON.

THAT'S WHEN I DECIDED TO GIVE FOUCAULT A GUIDED TOUR OF THE CITY'S VARIOUS BOOKSTORES, JUST SO I COULD GET HIS TAKE ON THE CURRENT TORONTO SCENE.

HIS ANSWER:

MY DEAR PETER, THIS CITY IS NOT NEARLY DECADENT ENOUGH FOR ME.

I WAS ALSO AUDITING A CLASS WITH SEMIOTICIAN UMBERTO ECO,...

...BUT WHILE ECO, LIKE FOUCAULT, WAS A BRILLIANT AND PATH-BREAKING SCHOLAR, NO CRITIQUES OF POLITICAL ECONOMY—SOMETHING I WAS IN DIRE NEED OF IN MY POLITICAL FORMATION.

I KEPT SEARCHING... SEARCHING HIGH AND LOW, AND FINALLY FOUND MY ANSWERS ONCE I WAS INTRODUCED TO THE WRITINGS OF PAULO FREIRE, JOSE PORFIRIO MIRANDA, CHE GUEVARA,...

...AND MOST OF ALL... KARL MARX.

READING KARL MARX HELPED ME QUESTION WHY THE UNITED STATES HAS THE LARGEST DEFENSE EXPENDITURES IN THE WORLD, THE HIGHEST LEVEL OF ECONOMIC INEQUALITY AMONG DEVELOPED COUNTRIES, AND THE WORLD'S GREATEST PER CAPITA HEALTH EXPENDITURES...AND, WHY—AMONG DEVELOPED NATIONS—DOES THE U.S. HAVE THE LOWEST LIFE EXPECTANCY. WHY DOES SUCH A RICH COUNTRY HAVE THE LOWEST MEASURES OF EQUALITY OF OPPORTUNITY? MARX EXPLAINS THAT IT'S BECAUSE WE LIVE IN A PLUTOCRACY. THE SUCCESS OF YOUNG PEOPLE TODAY IS PRIMARILY DEPENDENT ON THE INCOME AND EDUCATION OF THEIR PARENTS.

MARX REVEALED THE FORCES AND RELATIONS OF PRODUCTION THROUGH WHICH CAPITALISM EXPLOITS WORKERS TO CONSTRUCT MARKETS THAT ARE DESIGNED TO SERVE THE PRIVILEGED AND THE POWERFUL. MARX ALSO UNCOVERED THE MECHANISMS WHICH HAVE KEPT WEALTH UNEVENLY DISTRIBUTED. THE WAGES IN PLACES SUCH AS NORTH AMERICA ARE ABOUT THE SAME AS THEY WERE FOR SIXTY YEARS—WHILE THE RICH'S SHARE OF THE TOP ONE PERCENT HAS DOUBLED THAT OF THE BOTTOM NINETY PERCENT. DON'T BELIEVE THOSE BLOVIATING REPUBLICAN FOX NEWS COMMENTATORS THAT SAY IT'S BECAUSE OF THE LAW OF SUPPLY AND DEMAND DETERMINING INTEREST RATES, WAGES OR THE COST OF LIVING. THAT'S CRAP! WE THE PEOPLE ARE WAGE SLAVES. THERE'S JUST NO OTHER WAY TO SEE IT.

IT'S MORE THAN CHANGES IN TECHNOLOGY AND THE NEED FOR SKILLED WORKERS, IT ALL HAS TO DO WITH THE MARKET POWER OF LOCAL SERVICES WHO CAN RAISE PRICES HOWEVER HIGH THEY WANT. OUR DEMOCRACY IS A COMMODITY, PAID FOR BY THE RICH TO RIG THE ECONOMIC GAME IN WAYS THAT FAVOR *THEM*, SUCH AS ATTACKING UNIONS, WEAKENING ANTITRUST LAWS, AND THE BARGAINING POWER OF THE WORKERS. THUS, MAKING IT HARD FOR NEW ECONOMIC PLAYERS TO ENTER THE GAME. THIS IS THE EXACT OPPOSITE OF COMPETITION.

THE EXPERIENCE OF READING MARX WAS LITERALLY A REVELATION, AND HERE I WAS DRAWN TO THE REVOLUTIONARY MESSAGE OF JESUS. YOU CAN FIND WHAT I LEARNED IN MY OTHER BOOK, *PEDAGOGY OF INSURRECTION*— BUT LET THIS BE A WARNING TO THOSE TESTOSTERONE-DRIVEN EVANGELICALS WHO WORSHIP TRUMP AND HAVE STOLEN JESUS AWAY FROM THE SCRIPTURES:

THE OFFICIAL TEACHINGS OF MANY EVANGELICAL BIBLE COLLEGES FALSIFY THE GOSPELS SINCE IT'S CLEAR FROM READING THE BIBLE THAT JESUS MAINTAINS AN INTRANSIGENT CONDEMNATION OF THE RICH.

...AND IF YOU DON'T BELIEVE ME, ASK *HIM*.

I DON'T CONDEMN WEALTH IN THE ABSOLUTE SENSE, AS WHEN THE WEALTH OF THE WHOLE PEOPLE IS PRAISED IN DEUTERONOMY 28:1-14. BUT WHEN I SAY "HAPPY ARE THE POOR" AND "WOE TO YOU THE RICH," I'M ATTACKING THE FACT THAT SOME PEOPLE ARE POOR AND OTHERS ARE RICH. AS MIRANDA EMPHASIZES, "RICH" AND "POOR" ARE CORRELATIVE TERMS.
IF YOU WANT TO UNDERSTAND MY MESSAGE, THEN RECOGNIZE THAT I ADVOCATE LOVE, AND THIS ALSO MANDATES JUSTICE. I IMPLORE YOU TO CREATE A WORLD HERE ON EARTH WHERE THERE ARE NO RICH AND NO POOR- WHERE ECONOMIC RIGHTS REIGN SUPREME. YOU CONSTANTLY TALK ABOUT HUMAN RIGHTS BUT IGNORE ECONOMIC RIGHTS. HYPOCRITES!
I MEAN, IF YOU ACCEPT ME AS YOUR PERSONAL SHOULDER TO CRY ON THAT'S ALSO RESPONSIBLE FOR INEQUALITY AND INJUSTICE, THEN WHAT DOES THIS SAY? THIS GOES BEYOND WHETHER YOU VOTE DEMOCRAT OR REPUBLICAN. IT'S AT THE HEART OF THE STRUGGLE TO BE HUMAN. IT DOESN'T MEAN THAT A SOCIALIST COUNTRY IS MORE CHRISTIAN THAN A CAPITALIST COUNTRY, ESPECIALLY IF THAT SOCIALIST COUNTRY HAS A TOTALITARIAN GRIP ON THEM.
WHILE JUSTICE IS MORE THAN ECONOMIC, IT REMAINS THE CASE THAT ECONOMIC JUSTICE IS FUNDAMENTAL TO THE KINGDOM OF GOD HERE ON EARTH. YES, WE CAN PRAY FOR THE ETERNAL SALVATION OF OUR SOUL, AND THOSE OF OUR BRETHREN, BUT WE CAN'T IGNORE THE FACT THAT THE KINGDOM OF GOD IS AT HAND.
ONLY LOVE AND JUSTICE IN THE HERE AND THE NOW WILL USHER IN THIS KINGDOM, MADE POSSIBLE BY THE GRACE OF MY FATHER. THE NOTION THAT DIFFERENTIATING WEALTH IS AN UNDISPUTED FACT OF LIFE IS— OF COURSE— FALSE. IT'S ALL A LIE THAT WE'RE SPOON-FED EVERY DAY IN THE MEDIA.

70.

71.

IN MY YEARS AS AN EDUCATOR, WHY WERE THE KIDS SO UNCOOPERATIVE AND PRONE TO SUCH GRISLY ACTS OF VIOLENCE IN AND OUTSIDE OF THE CLASSROOM?

I SPENT A YEAR IN ANOTHER INNER-CITY SCHOOL IN DOWNTOWN TORONTO, WHERE MOST OF THE KIDS WERE EITHER ITALIAN OR AZOREAN.

BAD GENETICS WAS THE ONLY EXPLANATION I RECEIVED..."BAD SPERM", AS ONE TEACHER DESCRIBED IT.

I REALIZED THAT SOME OF THE TEACHERS HAD A "DEFICIT MODEL" OF THE STUDENTS, FOCUSING MORE ON WHAT THEY LACKED. THAT WAS A MODEL I GREATLY REFUSED. INSTEAD, I LOOKED AT THE RICHNESS OF THEIR EXPERIENCES AND BELIEVED THAT EDUCATION SHOULD START BY EMPHASIZING A STUDENT'S STRENGTH.

PART SEUEN

PROFESSOR

DAYS

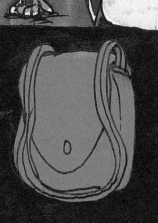

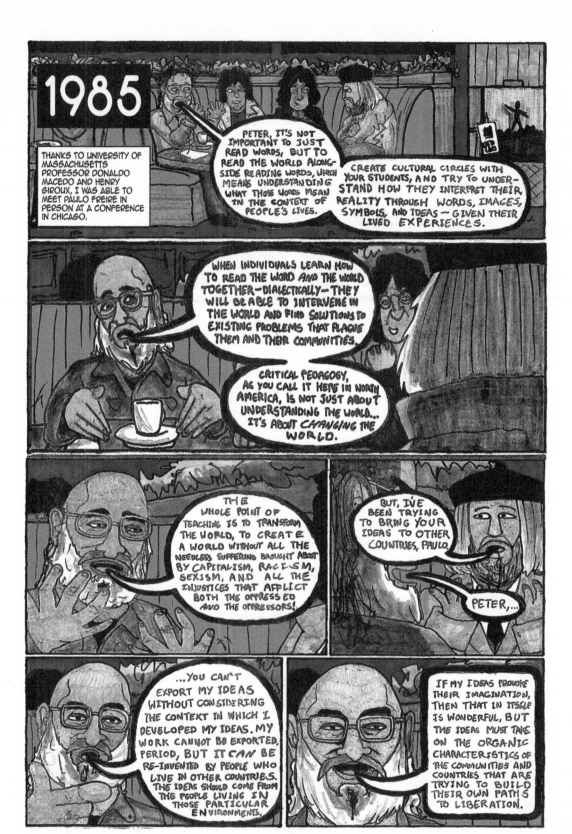

LATER, I WOULD MEET
ANTONIA DARDER, A CRITICAL
EDUCATOR WHO TAUGHT ME
THE IMPORTANCE OF FREIRE'S
WORK IN WORKING-CLASS
COMMUNITIES THROUGHOUT
THE UNITED STATES.

I TRAVELED TO ENGLAND A HANDFUL OF TIMES THROUGHOUT THE 1990S AND THE BEGINNING OF THIS CENTURY TO LEARN MORE ABOUT MARXISM FROM DAVE HILL AND MIKE COLE.

I FELT LUCKY TO HAVE SUCH GREAT MENTORS EARLY ON, INCLUDING HENRY GIROUX, WHO WAS A STRONG INFLUENCE IN MY THINKING ABOUT POLITICS AND PEDAGOGY.

PETER HUDIS—AN AMERICAN MARXIST—HELPED ME COMPREHEND MARX'S WORK IN LIGHT OF THE GEOPOLITICS OF THE CURRENT TIMES.

WILLIAM I. ROBINSON FILLED ME IN ON THE SHIFTS FROM GLOBAL CAPITALISM TO THE TRANSNATIONAL CAPITALIST STATE.

AS ROBINSON NOTED, A MAJOR DIFFERENCE BETWEEN TWENTIETH AND TWENTY-FIRST CENTURY FASCISM INVOLVES THE EMERGENCE OF THE TRANSNATIONAL CAPITALIST CLASS OVER THE PAST SEVERAL DECADES. FOR ROBINSON, TWENTIETH CENTURY FASCISM INVOLVES THE FUSION OF NATIONAL CAPITAL WITH REACTIONARY AND REPRESSIVE POLITICAL POWER. TWENTY-FIRST CENTURY FASCISM, HOWEVER, INVOLVES THE FUSION OF TRANSNATIONAL CAPITAL WITH REACTIONARY POLITICAL POWER.

TODAY'S RECOMPOSITION OF THE POLITICAL FORCES WITHIN CAPITALIST GLOBALIZATION REFLECTS OUR CURRENT STATE. IN ORDER TO UNLOAD THE TRILLIONS OF DOLLARS ITS ACCUMULATED, THE TRANSNATIONAL CAPITALIST CLASS HAS TURNED TO MIND-NUMBING PRACTICES OF FINANCIAL SPECULATION—FROM THE PILLAGING OF PUBLIC BUDGETS, TO WHAT ROBINSON REFERS TO AS "MILITARIZED ACCUMULATION." THAT IS, TO ENDLESS CYCLES OF WAR, DESTRUCTION, RECONSTRUCTION, ACCUMULATION BY REPRESSION, THE STRUCTURAL NECESSITY OF ENDLESS SURPLUS VALUE, PROFIT, AND THE CONSTRUCTION OF A SURVEILLANCE STATE.

MICHAEL PETERS ENCOURAGED ME TO UNDERSTAND KNOWLEDGE CAPITALISM AND ITS RELATIONSHIP TO HOW UNIVERSITIES FUNCTION.

I CROSSED PATHS WITH OTHER LEFTIST INTELLECTUALS FROM ALL OVER THE WORLD, ALL OF WHICH HELPED ME REFINE MY ATTITUDE TOWARDS POLITICS IN THE CONTEMPORARY ERA—INCLUDING FINNISH EDUCATOR JUHA SUORANTA...

...AND CROATIAN SCHOLAR PETAR JANDRIC. TOGETHER, WE EXPLORED NEW IDEAS IN CRITICAL LEARNING IN THE DIGITAL ERA—THOUGH IT BECAME CLEAR TO ME THAT AS FAR AS TECHNOLOGY WAS CONCERNED, I WAS DEFINITELY OLD SCHOOL.

77.

I MET JOE KINCHELOE—A BRILLIANT EDUCATOR FROM TENNESSEE—AND LEARNED SO MUCH FROM HIM... ENOUGH TO HELP ME DEVELOP MY PATH TO CRITICAL PEDAGOGY.

BERNARDO GALLEGOS AND SANDY GRANDE GAVE ME INSIGHT ON INDIGENOUS RIGHTS AND BECAME MY DEAREST FRIENDS...

...AS DID CARL BOGGS, WHO TAUGHT ME HOW THE POLITICS OF FASCISM IN AMERICA WORK.

79.

DURING VISITS TO BRAZIL, I MET A MAN WHO WOULD BECOME MY FATHER OF THE SAINTS NAMED MR. SEVEN. HE BELONGED TO A TEMPLE THAT WORSHIPS A DEITY KNOWN AS EXU AND THANKED ME WITH A PLAQUE FOR HELPING HIM DEFEND AFRO-BRAZILIAN RELIGION AGAINST STRICT CHRISTIAN EVANGELICALS WHO THOUGHT UMBANDA WAS INSPIRED BY EVIL...WHEN IN FACT, IT'S BEAUTIFUL—AND SOME CATHOLIC PRIESTS ARE UMBANDISTAS.

I EVEN PARTICIPATED IN UMBANDA CEREMONIES, WHERE I ONCE SAW MR. SEVEN SPINNING IN A CIRCLE LIKE A TOP WHILE HE WAS POSSESSED BY EXU.

IN FACT, LET'S TALK ABOUT *HIM* FOR A JUST A SECOND TO CLEAR SOMETHING ELSE UP, SHALL WE?

MANY PEOPLE THINK EXU IS THE DEVIL. HE'S NOT. HE JUST SIMPLY GUARDS THE CROSSROADS. WHENEVER BLUES SINGERS TALK ABOUT BEING "AT THE CROSSROADS", THEY'RE MOST LIKELY —IF NOT UNCONSCIOUSLY— REFERRING TO EXU. MR. SEVEN WOULD INVOKE EXU, BUT WOULD ONLY USE HIS POWERS FOR GOOD.

HE KNEW THAT BAD DEEDS WILL COME BACK AT YOU AND THAT YOU REAP WHAT YOU SOW.

I FREQUENTLY TRAVELED TO MEXICO IN THE MID 80S, BUT WHEN INSTITUTO McLAREN WAS GRANTED A CHARTER BY THE UNIVERSITY OF TIJUANA, I KNEW THAT I'D BE SPENDING A LOT MORE TIME THERE.

LATER, SERGIO QUIROZ MIRANDA—MY GOOD FRIEND AND DIRECTOR GENERAL OF INSTITUTO McLAREN—DECIDED TO BREAK FREE FROM THE UNIVERSITY'S RESTRICTIONS AND ESTABLISH INSTITUTO McLAREN AS A NON-UNIVERSITY AFFILIATED EDUCATIONAL INSTITUTION.

INSTITUTO McLAREN EVENTUALLY BRANCHED OUT INTO MICHOACAN, OAXACA, CHIAPAS AND JALISCO.

INSTITUTO MCLAREN

DE PEDAGOGIA CRIT

ENSENADA, BAJA CALIFORN

SOLIDARITY AGAINST WHITE SETTLER COLONIALISM

IDLE NO MORE!

TO MY SURPRISE, I WAS HONORED IN THE STATE OF CHIHUAHUA BY THE RARAMURI—OR TAHARUMARA—INDIGENOUS PEOPLE IN COPPER CANYON WITH A SPECIAL CEREMONY.

JUST TO BE HONORED AND ABLE TO MARCH ALONGSIDE THEM IN PROTEST MEANT MORE TO ME THAN ANY OTHER AWARD I'VE EVER RECEIVED OVER THE YEARS FROM ACADEMIC INSTITUTIONS. I SAY THAT NOT OUT OF DISRESPECT FOR THESE INSTITUTIONS—SOME OF WHICH ARE DOING IMPORTANT WORK TO THIS DAY—BUT OUT OF GREAT REVERENCE I HAVE FOR THOSE WHO TREATED ME SO KINDLY, DESPITE THE FACT THAT MY ANCESTORS MOWED *THEIR* ANCESTORS DOWN HALF A CENTURY AGO.

I WAS DEEPLY GRATEFUL TO MEET MARCOS AGUILAR, PRINCIPAL OF ANAHUACALMECAC INTERNATIONAL UNIVERSITY PREPARATORY HIGH SCHOOL OF NORTH AMERICA—FOR GRADES KINDER THROUGH TWELFTH. HE INVITED ME TO ACCOMPANY HIM TO A CONFERENCE ON INDIGENOUS RIGHTS IN MEXICO CITY, GAVE ME TOURS OF SACRED SITES...

...AND TAUGHT ME THROUGH THE EXAMPLE OF PEDAGOGIES OF WISDOM DEVELOPED AT ANAHUACALMECAC—LOCATED IN EAST LA—HOW STUDENTS OF ALL ETHNICITIES COULD SUCCEED AT BECOMING INTERNATIONALLY-MINDED, AND CULTURALLY RESPONSIVE ACTIVISTS FOR SOCIAL JUSTICE.

WE HAVE A LOT TO LEARN FROM OUR INDIGENOUS ANCESTORS. THAT HAS TO BE PART OF *ANY* CRITICAL PEDAGOGY, PETER.

I COULDN'T'VE AGREED MORE.

I WAS ALSO INVITED BY LEADERS OF THE PUREPECHA COMMUNITY IN CHERAN, MICHOACAN TO DISCUSS DEFENSE OF THEIR LANDS.

AROUND THAT SAME TIME, THE DRUG CARTELS WERE DIVERSIFYING AND MOVING INTO THE LUMBER BUSINESS, STEALING TREES FROM THE PUREPECHA PEOPLE AND SELLING THEM TO THE HIGHEST BIDDERS...

...BUT THE SELF DEFENSE GROUPS WERE QUICK TO PUT THEM OUT OF COMMISSION.

TRAVELING THROUGH LATIN AMERICA AND THE CARIBBEAN GAVE ME AN EDUCATION I COULD'VE NEVER RECEIVED FROM READING BOOKS.

SERGIO QUIROZ, MY WIFE WANG YAN, AND I VISITED COMMUNITIES IN CHIAPAS THAT WERE SUPPORTERS OF THE ZAPATISTAS— A GROUP I GREATLY ADMIRE.

NOT ONLY DID I GET TO MEET THE LATE-VENEZUELAN PRESIDENT HUGO CHAVEZ, BUT SERGIO AND I TRAVELED TO CUBA TO SPEND AN AFTERNOON WITH CHE GUEVARA'S DAUGHTER ALEIDA, WHO WAS KIND ENOUGH TO SHARE SOME OF HER FATHER'S PRIZED POSSESSIONS.

83.

PART EIGHT

DAYS OF RAGE

2006

I WAS RANKED UCLA'S MOST DANGEROUS PROFESSOR IN A LIST OF OTHER PROFESSORS THAT WAS CALLED "THE DIRTY THIRTY."

THE ORGANIZATION RESPONSIBLE FOR THIS LIST CALLED ITSELF THE BRUIN ALUMNI ASSOCIATION, A ULTRA-CONSERVATIVE GROUP THAT DEEMED ME A THREAT TO AMERICA'S YOUTH. I GUESS THEY DON'T WANT THEIR STUDENTS TO BE TAUGHT HOW TO THINK CRITICALLY,...

...AND APPARENTLY MY TRIP TO SOUTH AMERICA TO SUPPORT CHAVEZ AND HIS EFFORTS TO HELP THE POOR DIDN'T SIT WELL WITH THEM, EITHER.

OTHERWISE, WHY ELSE WOULD I BE GREETED BY A THRONG OF REPORTERS?

THE UNITED STATES TRIED TO TOPPLE CHAVEZ BY ORGANIZING A COUP WITH THE VENEZUELAN RULING CLASS. HELL, AMERICA HAS TRIED TO TOPPLE GOVERNMENTS ALL OVER THE WORLD THAT THREATEN ITS FINANCIAL AND GEOPOLITICAL INTERESTS.

THE BRUIN ALUMNI ASSOCIATION OFFERED TO PAY STUDENTS A HUNDRED DOLLARS TO SECRETLY AUDIOTAPE MY CLASSES,...

...AND FIFTY DOLLARS TO PRODUCE NOTES FROM SAID CLASSES.

PRETTY SOON, THE FBI RAN A CHECK OF THE LIBRARIES TO SEE WHAT BOOKS STUDENTS WERE CHECKING OUT.

THIS WAS THE SURVEILLANCE STATE IN FULL FORCE.

BECAUSE OF RICHARD, I WAS ABLE TO FORM A CLOSE FRIENDSHIP WITH JOEL KOVEL DURING THE LAST FEW YEARS OF HIS LIFE...AND IT WAS QUITE AN AMAZING ONE AT THAT. AMAZING AND EDUCATIONAL.

I WAS FORTUNATE THAT RICHARD KAHN— ONE OF MY FORMER STUDENTS—WAS ABLE TO DEVELOP A NEW FIELD OF EDUCATIONAL STUDIES CALLED "ECOPEDAGOGY" AND BECOME ONE OF ITS EARLY PIONEERS.

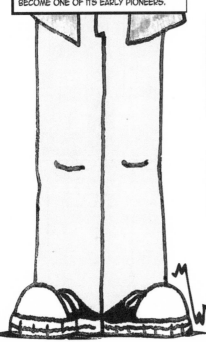

WHEN HE SERVED AS A PSYCHIATRIST AND WROTE THE BOOK *WHITE RACISM*, IT WAS A BREAKTHROUGH IN UNDERSTANDING RACISM FROM A PSYCHOANALYTIC PERSPECTIVE.

WHEN HE SHIFTED TOWARDS CHALLENGING THE POLLUTION OF OUR PLANET, HE HELPED DISCOVER THE ECO-SOCIALIST MOVEMENT.

KOVEL WAS BORN INTO A FAMILY OF JEWISH IMMIGRANTS FROM EASTERN EUROPE THAT FLED TSARIST UKRAINE—BACK WHEN THERE WAS A TWENTY-YEAR DRAFT FOR ALL JEWISH RECRUITS.

KOVEL'S FATHER LOU WAS ABLE TO SECURE A JOB AS AN ACCOUNTANT AFTER ESCAPING DNEPROPETROVSK AND MAKING THE LONG TRIP TO WILLIAMSBURG, VIRGINIA.

DESPITE LOU'S SPORADICALLY VIOLENT TEMPER, HE WAS STILL ABLE TO PROVIDE STABILITY AND SOME SENSE OF SECURITY WITHIN THE KOVEL HOUSEHOLD—ENOUGH TO SACRIFICE FINANCIALLY JUST SO HIS SON COULD ATTEND YALE.

KOVEL'S MOTHER ROSE ON THE OTHER HAND, ONCE BLAMED JOEL FOR GIVING HER BREAST CANCER...YET MAINTAINED A DEVOTED, LOVING SIDE TO HER THAT WAS LURKING WITHIN.

IN THE LONG RUN, HER IMPACT ON HIS LIFE PAID OFF, FOR IT BECAME ONE OF THE MANY THEMES IN HIS MEMOIR THE LOST TRAVELER'S DREAM.

KOVEL ATTENDED PS 99 ON EAST 10TH STREET IN THE MIDWOOD SECTION OF BROOKLYN, A SCHOOL WHOSE ALUMNI WOULD GROW UP TO BECOME HOUSEHOLD NAMES,...

...INCLUDING ALLEN "RED" KONIGSBERG—

—A.K.A. WOODY ALLEN.

PROMP

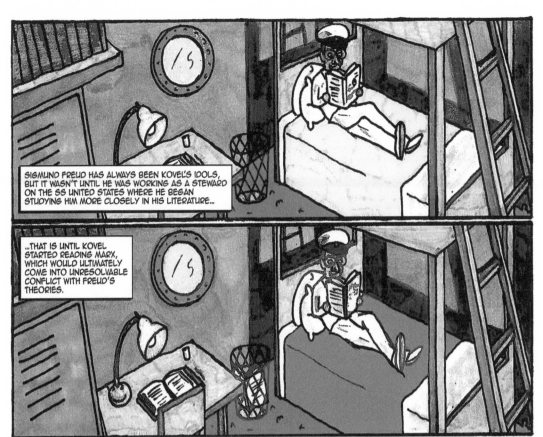

SIGMUND FREUD HAS ALWAYS BEEN KOVEL'S IDOLS, BUT IT WASN'T UNTIL HE WAS WORKING AS A STEWARD ON THE SS UNITED STATES WHERE HE BEGAN STUDYING HIM MORE CLOSELY IN HIS LITERATURE...

...THAT IS UNTIL KOVEL STARTED READING MARX, WHICH WOULD ULTIMATELY COME INTO UNRESOLVABLE CONFLICT WITH FREUD'S THEORIES.

HIS ENGAGEMENT WITH THE VAST CORPUS OF MARX'S WORK HELPED INSPIRE KOVEL'S POLITICAL REVELATIONS ON THE EARLY FORMATION OF THE NATIONAL SECURITY STATE AT A TIME WHEN JOHN FOSTER DULLES AND JOE MCCARTHY WERE WREAKING THEIR WORST POLITICAL HAVOC.

READING THROUGH *LOST TRAVELER'S DREAM*, IT WAS DIFFICULT NOT TO BE IMPRESSED BY THE VAST ARRAY OF WELL-KNOWN INTELLECTUALS, POLITICAL FIGURES AND ARTISTS THAT—AT ONE TIME OR ANOTHER—BECAME KOVEL'S PERSONAL FRIENDS AND COLLABORATORS.

FOR INSTANCE, KOVEL RECOUNTS ANECDOTES—MODEST AND UNEMBELLISHED—OF BEING INVITED BY THE KENNEDY ADMINISTRATION TO ATTEND A SPEECH GIVEN BY JOHN F. KENNEDY HIMSELF... JUST DAYS BEFORE THE CUBAN MISSILE CRISIS,...

...ATTENDING A LECTURE BY FIDEL CASTRO,...

...AND MEETING SOME OF THE MOST IMPORTANT LEFTIST PHILOSOPHERS OF THE DAY, INCLUDING RAYA DUNAYEVSKAYA.

DURING KEY POLITICAL EVENTS OF THE TIME, KOVEL WAS OMNIPRESENT. THUS, I WAS HARDLY SURPRISED TO LEARN THAT HE SERVED AS A COURTROOM DEFENDANT DURING A LAWSUIT INVOLVING MINIMALIST SCULPTOR RICHARD SERRA AND HIS TILTED ARC SCULPTURE THAT THE GOVERNMENT WAS TRYING TO REMOVE FROM THE FEDERAL PLAZA GROUNDS.

WHILE HOLDING SHORT-TERM POSITIONS AS A VISITING LECTURER AT SAN DIEGO STATE IN THE SPRING OF 1990—AND ANOTHER VISITING PROFESSOR POSITION AT UCSD IN WINTER THE FOLLOWING YEAR, KOVEL'S POLITICAL LIFE BECAME MARINATED IN THE MESSY WORLD OF REALPOLITIK.

HE RAN FOR THE U.S. SENATE WITH THE GREEN PARTY BEFORE TRYING TO SEEK THE PARTY'S PRESIDENTIAL NOMINATION IN DENVER,...

...BUT LOST TO RALPH NADER.

ON JUNE 20TH, 2009—A DECADE AFTER BEING APPOINTED ALGER HISS CHAIR OF SOCIAL STUDIES AT BARD COLLEGE, KOVEL'S ACADEMIC CAREER WOULD ALSO COME TO AN ABRUPT END...ONE THAT HE ANTICIPATED WOULD BE HASTENED BY THE PUBLICATION OF HIS BOOK *OVERCOMING ZIONISM* TWO YEARS PRIOR.

YOU SEE, KOVEL FAVORED A ONE-STATE SOLUTION TO THE BLOODY CONFLICT BETWEEN THE ISRAELIS AND PALESTINIANS. UNSURPRISINGLY, HIS ACERBIC CRITIQUE OF ZIONISM AND THE STATE OF ISRAEL WAS SEAMLESSLY CONFLATED WITH ANTI-SEMITISM —A CONUNDRUM THAT OFTEN MARKED THE END OF ANY DISSENTING PROFESSOR'S CAREER... EVEN ONES AS DISTINGUISHED AS KOVEL.

THE COMPLICITY OF ACADEMIC INSTITUTIONS IN THE CRIMES OF THE TRANSNATIONAL CAPITALIST STATE AND THE HYPOCRISY OF FREE SPEECH WITHIN SAID ACADEMIC INSTITUTIONS IS ALL UNEARTHED IN HIS BOOK.

2014

THOMAS C. WILSON, SUZANNE SOOHOO, LILIA D. MONZO, AND ANAIDA COLON-MUNIZ—ALL OF WHOM ARE MEMBERS OF THE PAULO FREIRE DEMOCRATIC PROJECT AT CHAPMAN UNIVERSITY—CONVINCED ME TO MOVE FROM UCLA TO CHAPMAN WHERE I COULD HELP THEM WITH THEIR AMAZING WORK IN BRINGING PAULO'S IDEAS TO THE STUDENT BODY AND ALL OF ORANGE COUNTY.

THE BEST PART ABOUT ALL OF THIS WAS THAT I HAD THE PRIVILEGE OF WORKING WITH WONDERFUL, DEDICATED ACTIVISTS AND SCHOLARS WHO ENCOURAGED MY INTERNATIONAL WORK.

LATER THE SAME YEAR, I WAS OFFERED THE POSITION OF DISTINGUISHED PROFESSOR AT CHAPMAN UNIVERSITY.

I WAS FINALLY AMONG OTHER PROFESSORS WHO WERE ALSO GUIDED BY PAULO'S WORK.

I'M STILL TEACHING AT CHAPMAN UNIVERSITY AND AT NORTHEAST NORMAL UNIVERSITY IN CHINA, HELPING TO BUILD COMMUNITIES OF SOCIAL JUSTICE EDUCATORS WHO WILL MOVE THE STRUGGLE FOR SOCIALISM FORWARD INTO THE FUTURE. WE MUST FIGHT FASCISM, ANTI-SEMITISM, RACISM, ABLEISM, SEXISM, HOMOPHOBIA AND THE COLONIALITY OF POWER AT EVERY TURN. NOW THAT'S WHAT I CALL CRITICAL PATRIOTISM.

2017

I MET BISHOP COLOMBO IN LA RIOJA, ARGENTINA AND HE SHOWED ME THE TOMB OF BISHOP ANGELELLI, WHO—ALONG WITH SEVERAL OTHER LEFTISTS AND ARGENTINIAN DISSIDENTS—WAS ASSASSINATED BY A MILITARY DEATH SQUAD IN 1976...

...ALL WITH HENRY KISSINGER'S PERMISSION NO LESS.

WHILE I PRAYED, I THOUGHT BACK TO EARLIER VISITS TO ARGENTINA WHERE I MET MEMBERS OF THE MOTHERS OF THE PLAYA DE MAYO, WHO SPENT DECADES PROTESTING THEIR FAMILY MEMBERS THAT DISAPPEARED "UNDER MYSTERIOUS CIRCUMSTANCES".

MADRES DE PLAZA DE MAYO
LINEA FUNDADORA

I KEPT HOPING THAT POPE FRANCIS WILL CONTINUE TO GIVE A BLOOD TRANSFUSION TO THE AIMS OF "THE PACT OF THE CATACOMBS"...

...A PLACE WHERE BISHOPS WOULD MEET IN SECRET AND PLEDGE SOLIDARITY WITH THE OPPRESSED.

I'VE SPENT SO LONG TRYING TO FIGURE OUT WHERE MY DRIVE TO EMBRACE LIBERATION THEOLOGY CAME FROM...

...AND THEN IT FINALLY HIT ME.

97.

98.

AHH, MID-TERM ELECTIONS. AT LEAST THE DEMOCRATS HAVE TAKEN BACK THEIR CONTROL OF THE HOUSE OF REPRESENTATIVES.

BELIEVE ME, I'M NOT A BIG FAN OF THE DEMOCRATS, BUT IF THEIR RESTORED INFLUENCE IS THE CLOSEST WE'LL COME TO A FIREWALL AGAINST TRUMPISM, WELL THEN I SUPPOSE THAT'S A COMFORT.

EXCEPT THEY HAVEN'T COMPLETELY CHASED THE MONSTERS AWAY JUST YET. THERE WERE SOME REPUBLICANS THAT WERE ELECTED, SUCH AS THE LATE-DENNIS HOF—AUTHOR OF *ART OF THE PIMP* AND WELL-KNOWN BROTHEL TYCOON. WITH STRONG BACKING BY CHRISTIAN EVANGELICALS, HOF WAS ABLE TO SLITHER THROUGH THE POLITICAL CRACKS AND WIN BY A LANDSLIDE— RECEIVING SEVENTY PERCENT OF THE VOTE IN NEVADA'S ASSEMBLY DISTRICT 36.

THEN THERE'S DENVER RIGGLEMAN. THIS *BIGFOOT EROTICA* ENTHUSIAST ONCE PROMOTED A BOOK CALLED *THE MATING HABITS OF BIGFOOT AND WHY WOMEN WANT HIM* AND WORKED AS AN AIR FORCE INTELLIGENCE OFFICER. NOW, HE HOLDS A HOUSE SEAT IN VIRGINIA.

I'LL GIVE YOU A MOMENT TO LET ALL THAT SINK IN.

DEMOCRACY IN THE U.S. IS CURRENTLY ON LIFE SUPPORT. WE NEED AN INFUSION OF DEMOCRATIC SOCIALISM AND TO START EXAMINING WHAT A VIABLE ALTERNATIVE TO CAPITALISM WILL LOOK LIKE. IT'S TIME TO STOP FALLING FOR THE SIMPLE, RHETORICAL COLD WAR TRICKS THAT WERE USED SO THAT PEOPLE WOULD HEAR THE WORD "SOCIALISM" AND CONJURE IMAGES OF NUCLEAR ANNIHILATION AND THOUGHT CONTROL.

DON'T FALL FOR THOSE FALSE EQUIVALENCIES THAT THOSE FAR RIGHT GUARDIANS OF CORPORATE MAGNATES CONTINUE TO RUN INTO THE GROUND. ALL THEY WANT TO DO IS STIR THE PUBLIC IMAGINATION WITH IMAGES OF SOCIALISM AS TANTAMOUNT TO A TOTALITARIAN DICTATORSHIP OR CRIMES OF NAZI GERMANY.

THE SOVIET UNION WAS NEVER COMMUNIST IN MARX'S TERMS,...

...IT WAS STATE CAPITALIST.

THE SAME COULD BE SAID OF THE FORMER EASTERN BLOC POLICE STATES. THEIR ECONOMIES WERE TIGHTLY CONTROLLED BY THE STATE—BUT WERE STILL CAPITALIST.

SO WHAT DOES "SOCIALISM" MEAN TODAY?